Open Adoption Open Heart

BOOK ONE of the *GLASS HALF-FULL ADOPTION MEMOIRS series*

BOOK ONE of the *GLASS HALF-FULL ADOPTION MEMOIRS series*

Open Adoption Open Heart

an adoptive father's
inspiring true story

RUSSELL ELKINS

Open Adoption, Open Heart: An Adoptive Father's Inspiring True Story
book one in the Glass Half-Full Adoption Memoirs series
By Russell Elkins
©2019 Russell Elkins

Chief line editor: Kim Foster
Content editors: Martin Casey, Cathy Watson Childs

Cover photo and author photo by Jammie Elkins Photography
Cover design by Inky's Nest Design
Interior book layout by Inky's Nest Design

ISBN: 978-0-9899873-7-0

Inky's Nest Publishing

RussellElkins.com
3rd edition
First edition printed in 2012 in the United States of America

To my beautiful wife, Jammie.
The best mother and partner I could have possibly hoped for.

CONTENTS

INTRODUCTION

ADOPTION, A MODERN PERSPECTIVE

When I was a young child in the 1980s and my family lived in South Carolina, our next-door neighbors adopted a baby boy. It was not too long afterward that the Navy transferred our family to California and we quickly lost contact with all of our South Carolina friends. Twenty-five years later, when my brother, Clark, found himself visiting South Carolina again, he went to our old neighborhood to take pictures of things he remembered from his childhood. While he was standing in the street in front of our old house, a young man from next door came out to see what he was up to. Clark realized immediately who this young man was and started to talk about the exciting day when his parents first brought him home.

"It was a lot of fun. The whole block was invited to the party," Clark said.

The young man shook his head, "I think you have me confused with someone else. I wasn't adopted."

"Oh," Clark said. "I just assumed since you look like you're in your twenties that the math lined up. It must have been a family that lived there before."

"No. My parents have owned this house for over thirty years. They have been the only ones to live here for that long."

"Well, then you have to be the guy."

"No. That's not me. I'm not adopted."

"Yeah, but..." Clark cut off his words when he noticed his wife squeezing his hand much tighter than usual and glanced over to see the look she was giving him. "Oh. Right. I must be thinking of someone else," and he quickly changed the subject.

Clark had only been six years old when we lived in South Carolina, so he had to wonder if his memory was incorrect. He called our parents when he got home that evening and, sure enough, he just had to be that adopted baby boy.

Clark felt terrible.

People did not typically speak as openly about adoption in the 1980s as they do now.

My wife and I knew very little about adoption when we first began to entertain the idea. We had wrongfully assumed that it was pretty much the same as when we were kids—when it was common to refrain from talking about it. It was not until we attended our first adoption orientation that we were introduced to the concept of "open adoption."

The terms "open" and "closed" adoption can have different meanings for different people. Typically, a closed adoption means the adoption agency (or someone else) decides on which home the child is to be placed. The biological parents and the adoptive family have no contact with each other.

Open adoption is a broad term that means there has been some level of contact between the biological parents and the adoptive family. In some cases, open adoption means the biological parents choose the couple without ever personally meeting them. In others, it can mean there is regular contact, such as exchanging photographs or visiting face-to-face.

Open adoption emerged in the late 1970s and early 1980s, but the idea was still considered radical. Few adoption agencies offered this option because many people still viewed the practice as an ongoing experiment. They did not know how this practice would affect the biological parents, adoptive parents, adopted children, or the adoption agency itself.

In many cases, the new concept of open adoption proved to be beneficial for all people involved. In studies done in the late 1980s and early 1990s, teenagers from open adoptions reported that they enjoyed having a larger support group (both adoptive family and biological family), felt they were more comfortable with their personal identity, and had a greater desire to know more about their biological family than did those who were adopted through closed adoption.

Caseworkers began to see the benefits of open adoption, but influence from biological parents was the biggest factor in agencies making open adoptions popular. Biological parents enjoyed the ability to help choose the home in which their child would be placed. They also enjoyed having a say in what type of contact they could have with the adoptive family after placement. And by the time the mid-1990s came around, it was more common for biological parents to choose to place their children with agencies that offered open adoptions rather than with those that did not.

Agencies that did not make the change struggled to stay afloat. With less biological parents choosing those agencies, the number of children placed through those agencies dropped. Also, upon seeing that birthparents preferred open adoption, adoptive couples became open to the new idea. The change was quick, and by the turn of the twenty-first century, open adoption had become the norm rather than the exception.

The concept of having contact with the biological parents was foreign to my wife and me as we began considering adoption, but as we discussed the pros and cons with our caseworker, we rather easily made the decision to choose open rather than closed adoption. We had decided long before we even first stepped into the agency office that we wanted to raise our child to embrace his or her roots rather than keep them secret (as was the case with that young man in South Carolina). We wanted our children to grow up proud of where they came from, and the concept of open adoption fit perfectly into that plan. We have never regretted our decision.

It was not quite as simple and easy as we thought it would be, though. Before a child is born, the biological parents have the only say in what happens with that child. That means that a couple hoping to adopt has the right to do little more than that: hope. Even if the hopeful adoptive couple is contacted early in the pregnancy, the biological parents have every right to change their mind about placing their child until formalities are finalized through the court system. That can be quite the stressful ride for an adoptive couple since almost all people who consider placing a child for adoption will second-guess their decision throughout the entire process.

Once an adoption is finalized, however, those tables turn.

After the biological parents dissolved their parental rights, the adoptive couple now holds all the power in the relationship. Most adoption agencies urge adoptive couples and biological parents to come to an agreement before the adoption takes place about the type of contact that will exist after placement. Some states even require that agreement in writing before the adoption can be finalized. But even if that agreement is reached, there are no legal ramifications if the adoptive parents go back on their part of the deal.

The difficulty lies in the fact that neither party really knows what they are getting into when they discuss the details of their agreement. Most of the time neither side had ever been in this position before. Even if they had, every adoption relationship is unique. These people typically know very little about one another when the adoption takes place and have had very little time to form what will end up being a very intense relationship.

Because of these factors along with many more, biological and adoptive parents often feel insecure until they figure out the new relationship. And even when they do a good job figuring out their relationship, aspects of that relationship often change quickly in an open adoption.

My wife and I would find ourselves facing internal battles we had not anticipated. It is not human nature to want to share the idea of parenthood with someone else. But we were determined to make our relationships work. We were determined not to be one of those couples who cut ties with our child's biological family just because things got tough.

Our road proved to be very bumpy and difficult, but it was also very much worth the ride. We would not change a thing if we could. It is the best thing that has ever happened to us. My wife and I are even closer now than we were before because we have learned new levels of love—both toward our child and toward our child's birth family. We embrace our roles as adoptive parents, and do not wish we had it any different. We love our unique family tree. We are proud of our family and hope to instill that same pride in our child. What a wonderful world we have discovered with open adoption!

1

FRUSTRATIONS WITH INFERTILITY

When my wife, Jammie, and I were first married, we used birth control. We were not waiting for anything specific before starting our family, but we did not want to start right away. As is the case with many newlywed couples, many people thought it was their place to give us unsolicited advice about when we should start having children. Some thought we should start immediately, and others told us we were crazy if we did not wait at least a few years.

About six months after we were married, while I was still in college, we decided to stop using contraceptives. We were not necessarily "trying" to start our family at that time, but we were happy to become parents if God sent a child to us. As the months went by, we gradually went from wondering if it would happen to hoping it would. It didn't happen.

After being married for about a year-and-a-half, I graduated from college and we moved to Boise, Idaho. We bought a house. We both started new jobs and began making friends. We were starting a new chapter in our life, and we began to really yearn to become parents. We started to try out some of the advice others had given us—even some things that were probably more superstitions and old wives tales than anything else. It didn't work.

Jammie started to keep a log of everything her body did. She kept a thermometer handy to take her temperature. She paid close attention to when her body felt unusual. She monitored everything she was expecting to happen. She took her blood pressure throughout each month. She wrote all of her observations in a small notebook she kept with her at all times. None of this seemed to help.

We started to play mind games with ourselves. We interpreted things the way we wanted them to be, thinking that any change in Jammie's body temperature or sickness in the morning might mean we were finally pregnant. Still, whether her period started early, on time, or late, the bad news always came.

Unpleasant feelings that accompany difficult situations usually soften with time, but that did not happen for us with infertility. With each month of disappointment, we did not become more accustomed to it. Quite the contrary, actually. Every month intensified our disappointment. We played more mind games with ourselves, trying to understand what we were doing so wrong to make God unwilling to send us a child.

It was not a secret around our social circles that we were struggling with this. Most people at work and those living on our street knew. Everybody at church knew our situation.

The problem was not that everybody knew, nor was it that so many people wanted to be sympathetic and help. The problem was that few people knew how to make us feel more comfortable in our situation. Some people avoided the topic all together, but many tried too hard to empathize.

Every year a handful of men at church would pressure me, trying to get me to go to a father-and-son campout. I did not want to go because I would either feel like I was camping alone or intruding on someone else's father-and-son time.

Each year on Mother's Day, Jammie would try to slip out of church quickly before someone could corner her, but every year people would track her down, thinking they were helping her feel better by pressuring her into receiving a flower.

Naturally, some people struggling with infertility would be hurt if they were not given a flower on Mother's Day or invited to a campout. Every couple reacts differently to the situation, and it is almost impossible for others to know how to act. What works for one couple may not be a good idea with another. There is no easy solution.

We did have a small group of people whom we allowed to be our true sympathizers. It was nice to have them along for the ride, even if they had never been in our shoes. They prayed with us. They hoped with us. They hurt with us. All were really close friends or relatives, but few of whom had actually struggled with infertility.

RUSSELL ELKINS

One of Jammie's friends who did relate was Natalie. Not only had she been told she would never be able to have children, but she was also a nurse at a fertility clinic. She spent her day at work helping people just like us. Jammie and Natalie were able to confide in one another. The biggest blessing of all, though, was that she shared her expertise. It was nice to receive advice from someone who knew the science of infertility, and had valuable experience instead of the well-intentioned, yet unsolicited, advice from people who thought the only reason for our infertility was because we ate the wrong foods.

We resisted visiting Natalie's office for a long time. Each month we ached and suffered from another month of infertility, but we still were hesitant. Finally, while out on one of our many walks, Jammie and I talked about how big of a blessing it was to have Natalie in our life, and we wondered why we were not taking advantage of the situation. I was reminded of the popular allegory where floods came and a man on his roof prayed for God to save him. Along came a boat, which he turned away, saying God was going to come save him. Then the same thing happened with a helicopter. After he drowned, he asked God in heaven why He did not come to save him, and God corrected him, saying that He sent the boat and helicopter. Jammie and I were sitting there, waiting for God to send us a baby the same way children come to most everyone else, but He was sending us a different lifeline. We were being stubborn, waiting for things to be done our own way, and on our own timetable. That is not how God works.

I got myself checked out first because we had been told it is a good idea to get the male's sperm tested early because it is an easy problem to diagnose.

I was pretty nervous about the visit because I thought that I was going to have to give a sperm sample in a public building. I pictured myself stuck at the doctor's office for hours while people knocked on the door asking if I was all right. I was relieved when they gave me the option of taking the test at home.

The test came out clean and healthy. But, was that good news or bad news? I suppose it was nice to know nothing was wrong with my body, but at the same time, it did not make us feel like we were any closer to solving our problem.

One positive thing that came out of it all was that I was able to give serious thought to how I would feel if I were to find out my body was the problem. I always told Jammie I would not look at her differently if we discovered that her body was preventing pregnancy, and I have never wavered from that. Waiting for my test results to come back solidified that way of thinking for me.

Jammie began her visits with Natalie by getting an ultrasound. Just like with my sperm test, her ultrasound showed that everything seemed healthy. Again, was that supposed to be good news? We were hoping to find some answers so we could either take a pill or inject some medicine, and the problem would be solved. Telling us that we were healthy just made us feel stuck in our progression.

Natalie got Jammie started on a series of shots to help boost the chances of getting pregnant. These shots also increased the likelihood that we could end up with twins or triplets. By that point, we were not too worried about the number, as long as we could have children. At that time, we had no real concept of how much work it would have been to have more than one baby. Yes, we were pretty naïve.

When the end of that first month came, we were on pins and needles. We knew which day Jammie was supposed to start her period, and we hoped it would not happen. It did. Still, just like had done before we started the specialized treatments, we tortured ourselves by wasting a few home pregnancy tests just to make sure.

During the second month—and I was not entirely sure why—I found myself having "that feeling." I felt convinced *this month is the month!* Natalie's magical shots were going to work. I was sure of it. I was convinced that Jammie was going to be carrying a little person inside of her after that month. I felt confident about it all month...up until her next period proved me wrong. As it turned out, my feelings were more desperation than inspiration.

The second month of treatments should have been easier on us emotionally since we had already been through the heartache once. It should have been, but it was not. It seemed reasonable to assume we would succeed during that second month since it was supposed to work that first month. Our emotional crash at the end of the second month was worse than that of the first.

We began the third month of shots. This time Jammie was much more optimistic than I was, though I did my best to keep that pessimism to myself. When her period came at the end of the month, even though I still hoped more than anything that I was wrong, I did not expect her to be pregnant this time. Again, the treatments did not work.

It was hard for me to swallow. There we were, sitting on the roof in the heavy rain. A boat came to save us from drowning. God had clearly sent us a lifeline, but I guess it was leaking or broken because it did not work. That did not make any sense. The ultrasounds and tests always told us everything was ideal for the treatments to work. I had felt so confident when we started the process that I was already making parental plans in my head. After all, we were not hoping for something unusual. We just wanted to do what many couples accomplish by accident. Still, after a few months of trying harder than ever before, and thus building up our hopes more than ever before, we were still stuck in the same place we had always been—just the two of us with only our two dogs to keep us company.

We had some decisions to make. Many people repeat the same process over and over and sometimes have results farther down the road, but we opted out. Three months of receiving the shots might not sound like a very long time, but when we were going through it, it felt like a decade. I admit our decision had a little to do with being somewhat strapped for cash, but if we had felt like it was the right road for us, we would have found a way. We definitely would have found a way.

We spent a lot of time on our knees in prayer, and we took a lot of walks together to talk things over. We felt it was time to jump ship and move on to something else. Years of infertility, topped off with some unsuccessful treatments, left us hungry for something different. There were plenty of other infertility treatments we could have tried, but we were finished. We were worn out. Each month made it harder and harder, and we felt like the road we were on was not leading us anywhere.

All of our friends had been excited when we started visiting Natalie's clinic. When we decided not to continue our treatments, however, some of those same friends were not too happy with us. Some people radiated their disapproval. They talked to us differently after that point, like we were foolish for quitting so quickly. One thing about personal revelation, though, is that it is personal. Jammie and I were in charge of our own situation, and we knew we were making the right decision for us.

Trials in life can sometimes be difficult to understand while we are right in the thick of things. In retrospect, I can now see how those trying times helped make us stronger. And even more important than that, looking back I can see how important those months were in helping us prepare for one of our true callings in life—being adoptive parents. Those hard times helped us to not only become ready to adopt, but to become *excited* to adopt.

2

THE QUEST FOR ADOPTION

I imagine that the decision to shift focus from infertility treatments to adoption would be a tough one for many couples, but it was not for us. When we talked about more infertility treatments, we felt exhausted and pessimistic. When we thought about adoption, those feelings changed to excitement and optimism. There was no glorious "aha" moment for us. It just felt natural to go with the option that brought us comfort and hope. And if the truth be told, I think part of the reason the prospect felt so much more comforting was because we thought it was going to be more predictable and promising. We soon found out that adoption is anything but predictable.

We began telling our friends about our change of plans, and about our newfound excitement for adoption. Many of those friends shared our enthusiasm, but there were others who thought we were "giving up" on having natural-born children.

They looked at our decision like we were settling for the next best thing, while we saw it as equally wonderful.

Some friends gave us suggestions of new things to try, making us feel as though they were hoping to save us from having to resort to adoption. They had a hard time understanding that we did not want to continue with any more miraculous medical procedures. We did not want try a new special diet that was sure to cure our infertility. We were not interested in using a surrogate mother. Our focus was now on one thing—adoption.

Most of our close friends paralleled our excitement, but not all. These friends viewed our glass as half empty rather than half full, while we chose to see our glass as filled to the brim. Once we decided that adoption right for us, we became excited almost overnight.

We chose an adoption agency, and attended a small orientation class. That was where we learned about open adoption for the first time. Even though we were not familiar with the term "open adoption," the concept made sense to us. We decided from the very beginning that an open adoption would be right for us.

In our orientation meeting, we learned about the requirements for adoptive couples, both with the agency as well as with the state. When we asked how long the process usually took, we were told that it depended upon how long it would take for expecting parents to choose us. Some couples get chosen within weeks while others wait five years or more.

The mountains of paperwork were tedious, but we worked hard on them and hammered it all out in about a month. It could have easily taken us much longer if we were not as motivated as we were. A caseworker came to our home to do our "homestudy," to make sure our house was safe and ideal for a child. We had our fingerprints and backgrounds checked. Jammie and I both got physicals from our local doctor. We shared our financial records with the agency. All of these things were done to show we were capable, ready, and trustworthy enough to take on a child.

Different states and adoption agencies have different requirements. With our situation, along with our paperwork and home inspection, we had to complete ten education hours. We attended local classes. We watched videos and read articles about the topics that most interested us. We traveled to an adoption convention in a different state where we completed more hours than we were required. We were so excited about adoption that we soaked in as much information as we could.

My greatest fear with the adoption process was the thought of coping with a failed placement. It pained me to think of becoming emotionally attached to a child, or getting my hopes up high, and then having something fall through. We attended a class that dealt with that very subject. I hoped the class would somehow reassure me and calm that fear, but I actually left it feeling worse than I did beforehand. I became more aware how common it is for adoptions to fall through. Our instructor had been through three such incidents, and she said that the feelings were very much the same as the times she had miscarriages with her natural pregnancies.

With all of our education hours completed, and after receiving approval from the agency and caseworker, our last step was to get our profile posted on the adoption agency's website. We spent a lot of time trying to get it just right. (I have included that letter at the end of this book for those interested in reading it)

We noticed that almost all of the couples' profile pictures were headshots. We did not want to look like just another couple. We wanted to stand out. Instead of a headshot, we wanted a picture that showed a little of our personalities. We chose to use a picture that showed us with our favorite hobbies—Jammie with her camera, and me with my acoustic guitar. We put a silly polka dot border around the picture to draw attention to it as well. Whether someone thought the polka dots were cheesy or not, we didn't care. Our goal was to catch someone's eye, and if that meant we needed to be cheesy then we were okay with that.

With our profile now online, all we could do now was to wait and hope. Having just finished so many hours of classes and mounds of paperwork, it was strange not to have anything to do. We used social media and other forms of communication to spread the word that we were adopting. We did have some thoughtful friends tell us they recommended us to someone considering adoption, but none of those referrals turned into anything. All we could do was wait.

Jammie and I believe very strongly in the power of prayer. At that time, my responsibilities at church were with the teenage boys, and Jammie worked with the teenage girls. We both spent a lot of time teaching and doing activities with the youth, so one Sunday we asked them if they wanted to help take part in a special day of prayer and fasting with us, specifically to help us with the blessing of being able to start our family. These young boys and girls were all very enthusiastic about being part of it, which made us feel very loved. When others also heard about our plan, they joined in as well.

My brother, Clark, and his family were the people closest to the whole situation. Clark is just eighteen months older than I am, and we grew up doing everything together. He moved here to Idaho and now lives just a few blocks away. He and his wife, Beth, had ached with us through our infertility, and they longed for the day when we could become parents almost as much as we did.

One day, about the time we finished our paperwork, they asked us to follow them into a separate room so we could talk in private. Jammie and I immediately suspected they were pregnant, and we were right. As was the case with most all of our friends, they were nervous to tell us, especially since, while it was a happy surprise for them, they were not trying for a fifth child when it happened.

I doubt they were worried we might be angry or resent them. However, they were justified in thinking we might be jealous or sad about someone else becoming pregnant. If this news had come to us a few months earlier, that may have been the case—although we would have still been excited for them.

Since we felt confident that were already on our own path to becoming parents, my brain quickly calculated the math. We were not only okay with the thought of someone else getting what we wanted, but we were also really excited about the idea that there was a chance we could have a child close in age to theirs. We smiled when we thought about these two kids possibly growing up together, stealing each other's toys, and knocking each other down. What could possibly be better than that?

3

THE LONG-AWAITED LETTER

Waiting was so very hard. The subject of adoption was never more than a millimeter from our minds. Every time we took one of our many walks, or while we ate dinner together, we could not seem to talk about anything else. It completely consumed us, similar to when we were trying the infertility treatments.

It was not happening as quickly as we wanted. Of course, our hopes of a quick process were not very reasonable. The average wait with our agency was about two years, and we had only been waiting a few months.

As if our need to wait was not painful enough, Jammie one day decided to hop onto the adoption agency's website to see how long it would take for our profile to show up. The agency we were using was a large one with hopeful adoptive couples all over the nation. We were heartbroken when our profile came up as number 851 out of 921 couple profiles. All of a sudden, we felt like small fish in a very big ocean. How could someone possibly choose us? How would they ever find us? Our hope of having a child close in age to my brother's baby suddenly felt impossible. We felt completely helpless again, just like when infertility treatments let us down.

Less than a week after Jammie had done that search something happened that changed everything. We suddenly didn't feel so hopeless anymore. We were no longer such small fish.

We got contacted by an expecting mother!

We were thrilled.

The e-mail she sent was short and simple, and it read like this:

Hi, My name is Brianna. I am 15 years old. I live in Mississippi and I am almost five months pregnant. I was looking at profiles and yours kind of jumped out at me. I have always wanted a baby and it hurts to have to give that up, even if it is my own decision. I know I can't give it what it needs when it comes to having both parents, and I have to do what is best for my baby. Anyway, I would love to talk to y'all about maybe adopting. Please e-mail me back.

Thank you, Brianna

Words cannot describe our feelings. Jammie was beside herself with excitement, but I was hesitant. I guess I tend to be the kind of guy who thinks that if it sounds too good to be true, it probably is. I do not like getting my hopes up just to be shut down, so my brain went quickly to pessimist mode.

I wondered if we were the only couple she had contacted. I knew that if I were in her position, I might contact a few different couples, and then choose between them.

I also wondered if there was a scammer on the other end of this e-mail just claiming to be a fifteen-year-old girl. Most adoptions take place within the biological parents' home state, so being contacted by someone outside of Idaho caused me to feel suspicious. Plus, we had heard a few horrible stories about how adoptive parents are purposefully led along, giving gifts and money, only for the potential birthparents to have a change of heart after a lot of hospital bills and expenses were paid for. Fortunately, there are laws in place to protect hopeful adoptive couples from that type of thing, but it still happens.

We wanted to write Brianna back immediately, but we were nervous that we would say the wrong thing. We decided to ask our caseworker, Jon, for advice. His initial thoughts were similar to mine. Even without telling him about my concerns, he wondered if it was a scam. He told us to go ahead and reply to her e-mail, and he would investigate into the background of the situation.

Jammie and I both wrote separate e-mails, and sent them together. We wanted her to see our individual personalities as well as show her that we were both interested and invested in this adoption.

Not long after sending her the e-mails, Jon called us back. He had talked to some caseworkers in charge of the agency in Mississippi, and there was not anybody named Brianna on their list of expecting mothers. We felt let down, but Jon counseled us not to worry because it was common for an expecting mother to contact a hopeful adoptive couple from their website before contacting the agency.

Brianna replied to us within a few hours, and we exchanged a few more e-mails the same day. We had been advised by people to keep our last names a secret—at least for a little while—but that secret was blown after just a few e-mails when we accidentally left our last name and contact information at the bottom of a letter. Oops. The next thing we knew, Brianna found us on Facebook and requested a link to our personal pages. We were excited and nervous all at the same time.

A lot of people also advised us to keep some emotional distance between us and the expecting parents, but even though it had only been a few hours since she first contacted us, we found ourselves excited to connect with her through Facebook anyway. We did, and that was where we got to see a picture of her for the first time. I was surprised when I saw her photo. For some reason, and I do not know why, I was expecting her to be African-American. For months I had been having a recurring dream in which we would adopt an African-American boy. The dreams felt so real that I guess I came to expect it to become true, and I was surprised when she turned out to be Caucasian. I was not glad or disappointed in the change—it was just different.

Not only were we able to look through her Facebook profile, but we also spent a few hours chatting on Facebook's instant messenger.

We discussed some things she needed to do in order to get in contact with the adoption agency. She soon did, and a Mississippi caseworker contacted Jon shortly afterward. The situation was real. It was exciting. Both Jammie and I hardly slept that night. We rolled and tossed and turned. I am usually a really good sleeper, but I actually slept better the night before Jammie and I got married than I did that night.

We were too excited to keep this news a secret. We immediately started telling our friends, and the news spread like wildfire among everybody we knew. In no time at all, everyone around us buzzed with excitement.

The spark from Brianna's first letter ignited us in every way. Over the next few weeks her letters and words continued to feed the fire, but as time went on, we could see those flames slowly burning out. After only a month had gone by, we were left with just embers. Everything on her end was becoming increasingly more complicated, and it did not look like the adoption would happen. We eventually lost hope.

Even though we had our hopes up so high, the loss came so gradually that the pain was not nearly as severe as stories we had heard, nor could we say it compared to a natural birth miscarriage like others talked about. Still, we were sad. We were back to square one with just our two dogs to keep us company.

Brianna had tried to discuss adoption with the biological father, Daren, but he did not want to hear it. He was more

33

interested in discussing marriage and raising the child together, but at age fifteen Brianna did not feel ready to be a wife and a mother. Neither of them wanted to budge from their position, and they found themselves at an impasse.

Brianna soon broke up with him, but Daren was not yet ready to let their relationship go. The only time he was willing to talk about the baby was when he was trying to use it as leverage to convince her to come back to him. When she refused to rekindle the relationship, he turned on her, spread rumors about her and sent her nasty e-mails.

Even when he seemed to have given up on rekindling his relationship with Brianna, he still refused to consider adoption. He made no attempt to help her with the pregnancy, whether emotionally or financially. He showed no interest in the child. In essence, he was telling her that he had no interest in caring of the child himself, but he wanted to be able to observe from a distance.

Without both signatures, the state of Mississippi would not allow Brianna to choose adoption. Brianna was the youngest of her siblings, and the last one still living at home. Her father lived on the other side of town, and her mother's job kept her out of the home most of the time, usually working through the night. Since she was not willing to marry Daren, it looked like the only choice for Brianna was to drop out of high school to raise this child on her own.

What a situation to be in! As sad and disappointed as Jammie and I were, Brianna was even more heartbroken. She was a straight-A student with plans of college and aspirations of someday becoming a nurse, but she found herself painted into a corner. She refused to even consider an abortion, so she had no other choice but to put those dreams on hold.

When we were first contacted by Brianna, our friends were so excited for us that the news had spread like wildfire. Once things fizzled out, we found that our friends were not so quick to spread the word. It seemed like every person in our social circle wanted an update, and we had to retell our bad news everywhere we went.

We were back to the drawing board—back to where we found ourselves as couple 851 out of 921 amazing profiles.

How frustrating.

4

BACK TO THE DRAWING BOARD

Very soon after we lost hope in our situation with Brianna, my cousin, Radene, called me. She was living in Pittsburgh, and she told me about a conversation her husband just had with their friend, Melissa. Melissa was a single mother in her 30s who just found out she was pregnant for a second time, and she was considering adoption for this child. Radene directed her to our personal blog, and gave her our email address.

Melissa soon reached out to us, and here is part of the e-mail she sent us:

> *I have known for a long time that this was not my baby to keep. I mean, I kept my daughter when she was born, even though I knew she wouldn't have a father in her life. I'm glad I made that decision and I stand by it, but still, this time it's different. I've pretty much known all along*

that this baby was meant for someone else. I know that—and not just because I have always felt a little guilty that my daughter doesn't have a father to help raise her.

Still, even though I knew this baby wasn't going to be ours to keep, I've been hesitant about something. I chose a couple in Kentucky that I liked, but I haven't been able to commit to them and now I think I know why. After talking to Justin and reading your profile online, I now feel that you are supposed to be my child's parents. I wondered for so long why I couldn't feel right about making the decision, and now I know. I'm so glad Justin introduced me to you guys.

It's hard to really get to know a couple by reading their profile. I mean, how can I really know if people are being honest just by reading something they wrote? Every couple's profile makes them look so wonderful. So with you guys, it's nice to know that Justin and Radene have known you for so long, and I trust what they say.

I have some questions for you about how open you want the adoption to be. Is it okay if we have some contact? We won't be intrusive—just some pictures would be nice—and let us write a letter to the child once in a while, too. And Jammie, I was wondering if you would like to be in the delivery room when the child is born. Also, would you like to know the sex of the child once I find out?

I look forward to hearing from you soon. You are an answer to my prayers. Melissa

We wrote back with a few questions, and waited for her response. It had been a little more than a month since Brianna first contacted us. Even though Melissa's letter seemed more definite and promising, Jammie and I did not feel quite the same level of excitement we had with Brianna's email. Was it because this was not our first time receiving contact? Or was it because we were protecting our emotions from more disappointment? Perhaps it was from another reason altogether.

Everything with Melissa made more sense when looking at it from a distance. Her letter showed us how firm she was in her conviction. It felt good to have something that appeared so solid. Still, for some reason, Jammie and I felt drawn to Brianna. I felt bad about having those thoughts. There we were, likely to become parents because of Melissa's selflessness, but for some reason we still found ourselves thinking about Brianna more than Melissa.

Brianna contacted us again. We had never stopped interacting with each other, but since the situation seemed hopeless and our options limited, we mentally resigned ourselves to the thought that she would raise the child. When she wrote us this time, she told us she was soon to get an ultrasound, and would then find out the baby's sex. Most interestingly, she still talked like she was hoping to find a way to make this adoption happen. She would not give up, so we continued to hold on to a small piece of hope, even though we could not see how she could convince Daren to sign the papers.

On the other hand, Melissa was planning to place a child with us as well. We did not know what to do, so we just waited.

There was not much else we could do. We did not want to rush into any major decisions. What would happen if we told both expecting mothers that we wanted both babies? We could possibly end up with two babies, just weeks apart, which would be almost like having twins. Or we could possibly scare both expecting mothers away.

It felt like a long time before we made any kind of decision, but it was only a few days. Brianna wrote us again and told us about her ultrasound. She bought us a nice card, which she sent to us through the postal service along with the ultrasound picture. The results were not completely clear, but they believed this child was going to be a boy.

Brianna's due date was moved up a whole month after the ultrasound. Not only was the baby arriving much earlier than previously expected, but the new due date was the exact same day that Clark and Beth were expecting their baby to be born. Melissa's baby was due about a month later than that.

Our emotions were all over the place, so we set up another meeting with Jon, our caseworker. He was well experienced in dealing with a lot of crazy situations, but ours was new to him. Normally, after an adoptive couple is contacted and chosen by an expecting mother, their adoption profile is removed from the agency's web page so they are not chosen again. Our situation with Brianna had never been solid enough to have our profile taken down, and our second contact was from an inside contact, so we were in a unique position. Jon discussed it with some influential people within the agency, and they ultimately decided we could adopt both babies as long as both expecting mothers were both okay with the idea.

We were not sure how we wanted to go about asking Brianna and Melissa. In fact, we were not really sure we could even handle two babies. We did feel, however, that the problem would probably iron itself out. Brianna's situation seemed hopeless with Daren's refusal to sign, and there was nothing anybody was going to be able to do about it. Plus, we still felt confident that Melissa was going to place her baby with us. That would be that. Everything would work itself out, right?

It was not that easy.

We decided to first ask Brianna what she thought about us adopting both babies. We wanted to ask her first because if we were going to scare someone off, we figured it might as well be the expecting mother with the impossible legal issues. If it scared her away, then it was never meant to be, and we would not even have to bother Melissa about it.

Our question did not scare Brianna away, though. Actually, she was really excited about the possibility. She loved to think her baby would have a sibling so close in age.

We then wrote Melissa an e-mail and waited. We could not do much more than wait since everything hung on what she would want to do.

She did not write us back.

We wrote a few other letters in hopes of getting something in return, but Melissa never did write us back. We called my cousin, Radene, to see if she knew what was going on, but she never had any new information. Even though Melissa was so convinced in her first e-mail that we were the right couple for her child, she changed her mind. We were not sure if it was our

41

question that scared her off, but she chose to place her child with a different couple. She never did write us back.

Since our situation seemed to be drastically different every week, our friends were always ready for an update. Our life was not usually so dramatic. One minute Brianna wanted us to parent her child, and then she did not have a choice. Next, Melissa wanted us to raise her child—then they both wanted us—then just Brianna. If I had not already gone bald, I am sure my hair would have fallen out.

Even though Jammie and I doubted the adoption would take place, Brianna still held onto her hopes. She still hoped to figure something out.

Then someone suggested she look into the adoption laws for Idaho where Jammie and I live. Laws vary from state-to-state, and Idaho has different regulations than Mississippi. In Idaho, the biological father cannot stop an adoption by simply refusing to sign the papers. In Idaho, if he is not interested in parenting the child himself, he could not stop her from choosing adoption. Most importantly, if the baby was born in Idaho, then the situation would be subject to the laws of Idaho, not of Mississippi.

Brianna discussed the possibilities with her mother and caseworker, and the next news we received blew us away.

Brianna was coming to Idaho. And since her doctor did not want her traveling during the last two months of her pregnancy, she would be arriving in less than a week!

5

SOLVING A BIG PROBLEM

Brianna was coming to our home state of Idaho to have her baby. She was only fifteen-years-old, and had never traveled very far away from home—especially not without the accompaniment of an adult. Since her mother's job would not allow her to come until shortly before the baby was due, Brianna would be traveling alone.

Brianna had never flown in a plane. Through the generosity of a friend who worked for an airline, Jammie and I had access to some standby tickets. We did have to still pay for the tickets, but they were at a significantly reduced price, which was a wonderful blessing. But standby tickets posed some new challenges that made us nervous. Our local Boise airport is somewhat small, and there were no direct flights all the way here. We did not want her to have to worry about connecting flights or other complications for an inexperienced flyer (especially since it was close to Christmas), so we booked a one-way flight to the nearest big city, Salt Lake City, Utah, which was a five hour drive away, and we went to pick her up there.

Brianna had a cell phone, but at the time her plane was supposed to land, our attempts to call went straight to voicemail. Naturally, our minds started to rummage through all the possibilities of what could have gone wrong. Did her standby tickets get her bumped to a different flight than we first expected? Was she still up in the air somewhere and that was why her phone was off? If so, how would we know when she was going to land? How would we ever find her? We had seen a few photos of her, but we were not positive we would recognize her when we saw her in person.

Since Brianna was a minor, Jammie received permission from the airline to meet her at the arrival gate. She set off to search for her while I waited near the baggage claim area. We figured she would stand out, so Jammie wandered the terminals until she found someone who resembled Brianna's photo—a young pregnant teenager standing alone. When she asked her name, she was not Brianna. What were the odds of that happening?

Jammie abandoned her search and joined me near the baggage claim area. From our vantage point we could not see the top of the escalator, so each passenger appeared gradually as they descended. As the congestion of travelers began to thin out, we saw a lone female passenger begin to descend wearing a pair of warm winter boots. Her pregnant belly then appeared.

Finally, the face we clearly recognized from her photographs came into view. This time we did not have to ask her name. She rushed over to us for a hug.

She had arrived.

We ate lunch at my sister's place, who lived close to the airport. Brianna was able to get a much needed nap and spent the evening walking around downtown Salt Lake City, which was beautifully lit up for the Christmas season.

We finished our evening off at my uncle's house to get some sleep before heading back to Idaho in the morning. Everything was running pretty smoothly, considering that the whole situation was rather overwhelming for Jammie and me, and especially for Brianna. She handled it much better than I would have when I was fifteen.

Brianna's arrival to Utah changed a lot of things back home in Mississippi. She had been worried that her complicated situation would become even more complicated the more others found out, so she asked her mother and siblings not to tell her father, who lived on the other side of town, or the rest of their extended family until she made it out west with us.

About the time we were sitting down to dinner at my uncle's place in Salt Lake City, Brianna's mom was on the phone with Brianna's dad telling him where she was, and about her adoption plans.

I awoke that next morning on an air mattress in my uncle's living room to the sound of Jammie's cell phone. I did not recognize the out-of-state number and I had to wonder who would be calling at such an early hour. It was Brianna's mother calling, and she was frantic. She had been trying to call Brianna's cell phone, but it was turned off.

After Brianna's father heard the news the day before, he spent all evening thinking about how he could get Brianna back home. He hated the idea of his daughter being on the other side of the country with a bunch of strangers at such a time. He wanted her home immediately.

We did not know Brianna's dad. We had never talked to him or exchanged e-mails. We did not know how he would react. The only thing we knew was that Brianna was worried he would not be on board with the idea, and she was worried he might try to stop her. She was right.

I felt bad for him. I could not help but wonder if I would react just the same if I were in his shoes.

While Jammie and I were downstairs in my uncle's kitchen nervously eating cereal, Brianna was upstairs talking to various people on the phone about why she was making these decisions. We were not part of any of those phone conversations. We did not know if her dad would successfully talk her out of the decision she had made. We did not know if her father would show up at our doorstep the next day demanding she come home. Everything was up in the air. We could only worry, wait, and hope.

Normally, the more I think about something out of my control, the more anxious and worried I get. That was not the case that day though. As nervous as I was, I still felt a sense of peace. It was as if a voice inside was telling me that it had been a miracle to have made it this far in our story, and it was not all going to have been for naught. My rational brain was trying to tell me this new dilemma was at least as serious as anything else we had faced, but my heart was telling me it would all work out. I did not know how, but I knew somehow it would happen.

About the time we stopped for lunch along the interstate to Boise, Brianna's siblings sat down to lunch with their dad to discuss Brianna's situation. They were all on Brianna's side, and while I do not think the talk over lunch changed his mind, it did soften his heart.

About the time we sat down for dinner back home in Idaho, Brianna's dad was having a heart-to-heart talk with his sister about a time she found herself in a similar situation. Brianna's aunt had become pregnant at a very young age, and she raised her baby as a single teenaged mother. While she very much loved the child she had raised, she shared with him some of the struggles that Brianna would have to face if she raised this child on her own. Her opinion was that if adoption was what Brianna wanted, he should not stand in the way.

Brianna's siblings and aunt were a strong force in favor of the adoption, but they were not the only ones weighing in on the situation. Other relatives were very much against the idea and they made sure her father knew it. Brianna's aunt and uncle felt very strongly that the baby should stay in the family and they insisted they be allowed to raise it, but Brianna had already considered them and decided against the idea.

When Brianna's father called her the next day, his words were a wonderful surprise. He had spent the entire night searching his thoughts. He had come to the conclusion that he was willing to accept Brianna's decision. Actually, he was not only willing to accept it, but he decided from that point on that he was going to be a support. He was as good as his word. From that day forward he stood behind her. He gave all of the love and support a man could give his daughter from so far away.

It was even better than we could have hoped for. We felt optimistic, like things were now going to continue on track. Everything would have been much more difficult for Brianna without the support he gave from that point on—especially now that Brianna was a pregnant teenager in a strange home and without any local friends.

6

AN INTERESTING SOLUTION

When Brianna had first contacted us months earlier, we told everyone the news that a baby could possibly be coming our way. Jammie and I had shared updates with people everywhere we went. At that time, we had never expected any of our friends to ever meet Brianna. When we found out Brianna was coming to Idaho, we worried she might feel uncomfortable knowing that so many strangers knew so much about her. We worried that every eye at church would follow her as people stared and whispered. People tend to do that no matter what church or social group they belong to. It is human nature.

Since Brianna showed interest in going to church with us, we shared with her these concerns and asked if she would prefer we attend somewhere else for the time being. We quickly realized that we were much more worried about it than she was. We drove the point home that people may do something to make her uncomfortable, but she insisted it was not going to be a big deal. Besides, the plan was for her to be with us in our home for only a week anyway, just until after Christmas, and then she would stay with someone else for a few months until it was time to return to Mississippi.

Once Brianna was with us in our home, there were a lot of things that needed to be taken care of. Brianna needed help setting up some doctor appointments. Brianna was still a minor, and because a lot of medical things (as well as other things) could go wrong, and her parents would not be there to sign, it was best that we got a lawyer to draw up some paperwork for us to have temporary guardianship. Brianna also needed to meet with her new caseworker at least once every week. She was able to attend a support group once a week for birthmothers, expecting mothers and single mothers. Jammie took care of the majority of these appointments along with many other things Brianna needed accomplish.

Jammie was all over the place with all of the aspects of the adoption as well as caring for a teenager. Many of the things that needed to be done had to be taken care of while I was at work, so I was not usually able to help. Other than a few things here and there, my schedule carried on pretty much like always. Jammie was the one who had a whole new busy schedule.

Our plan for Brianna to stay in our home for just a week got stretched to two weeks, then to three weeks, then longer. We had more than one generous family express a willingness to let her stay with them, but with all of the new responsibilities on Jammie's shoulders and the busy schedule, it just became easier for Brianna to stay under our roof. Plus, we had always considered it an option to have her stay with us the entire time, but we did not want that to be our primary plan in case something went wrong or was too uncomfortable.

It was hard to predict how things might go with a guest for two months, especially when the guest was almost a complete stranger. Things were going well though. Considering she was only fifteen, had no local friends her age, was pregnant, did not have a whole lot of enjoyable things to occupy her time during the day, had the hormones of pregnancy, and was far away from her family, she seemed to be doing rather well with the situation. Sure, some days were tougher on her than others, but she was a real trooper. She responded well above the age level of what I would expect from a typical fifteen-year-old.

Our caseworker, Jon, wanted to make sure everything with our situation was done by the book. He wanted to make sure Daren had the ability to choose to parent this child if he wanted to, and wanted to make sure our situation could not appear like we were hiding Brianna or the baby from him.

We had heard stories about birthmothers who had gone to other states in order to hide from the biological father, often lying to him about the situation until after the adoption was finalized. We did not want our situation to appear like that. We did not want to lie to Daren. We did not want to cheat him out of a chance to raise his son if that was what he wanted to do.

Jon asked Brianna to start some correspondence with Daren in order to create a paper trail to prove everything had been done legally and honestly. She began by writing him a simple letter, telling him where she was and what she was doing. This information was not going to be new to him. He already knew she was with us in Idaho, but we felt it was important to have it on record. She sent it via certified mail in order to have proof that he received it. After some time passed and he did not respond, she sent him a text message asking if he got it, and he replied that he had.

Over the course of a week, Brianna and Daren exchanged text messages, all of which we kept for our records. Their new correspondence seemed to have rekindled in Daren a desire to be together again. Much like he had done while she was still back home, he rarely mentioned her pregnancy or the baby, and when he did, he it was done so only as leverage to say he thought they should get back together. When she refused, he began again to call her names and turned nasty toward her. Their correspondence ended when he told her wished she would just go away and not contact him anymore.

Jammie and I knew very little about Daren, and the only things we did know were not flattering—the way he treated her during that week of correspondence, his legal troubles with drugs and school, and so forth. Even though he was not interested in raising this child, we still planned to keep him as part of our open adoption if that was what he wanted. We were not likely going to invite him to our home, but we told him we would be happy to send him updates and pictures.

***

We found a lot of joy in having Brianna in our home. It was fun to really get to know her, and it was fun for her to get to know us. I can only imagine how an expecting mother would constantly wonder if she was choosing the right family for her baby. Any hopeful adoptive couple can make a beautiful online profile and include a bunch of flattering pictures, but actually getting to know the adoptive couple as well as she got to know us was something few expecting mothers get to experience.

The relationship between biological parents and adoptive parents is not a natural one. It is not instilled in us as human beings to naturally want to share the idea of parenthood with someone else. Since we were not giving birth to this child, it could have felt natural to feel a sense of competition for the title of "parents."

We had a lot of emotional and difficult times coming our way, and getting to know Brianna on such a personal level in our home helped us see her as the beautiful girl that she was rather than as competition. She was someone we truly came to love, and not just because she was giving us the gift of parenthood, but because we knew her as a person and loved her as our own. The pull for us to compete with her was always overshadowed by our love for her. We will always be grateful for that.

7

BECOMING REAL

One of my friends adopted a son a few years earlier. He flew all the way out to St. Louis to bring the new baby home, but the biological mother changed her mind after the child was born. He and his wife flew home empty-handed. He cried for two weeks straight before they got a surprise phone call from their caseworker telling them the biological mother reversed her decision and the baby would be coming to their home after all.

I think it was partly because of his story and others like it that I was afraid of becoming completely invested emotionally only to be heartbroken if our adoption fell through. With each hoop we jumped through, every new experience with Brianna during her pregnancy, every day that passed and we came closer to her due date, I felt a bit more invested. Still, I reserved a part of myself in order to avoid total heartbreak. I, like many people, have had my heart broken after committing myself to a relationship, and the trauma from those instances caused me to keep myself more guarded when entering new relationships.

With this in mind, there was one thing that I had wanted to do ever since Brianna showed up in our home, and it took me a few days to build up the courage. One evening, while Jammie and I were watching a movie with Brianna, I noticed she had her hand on her belly to feel the baby kick. That was what I wanted to try. After asking her permission, I held my hand on her stomach for a moment, just long enough to feel a few kicks. I wondered if the experience would lock me in to "fully invested" mode with my emotions, but it did not. Maybe it was because I was uncomfortable touching the belly of a woman who was not my wife. Still, even though I felt fairly confident the adoption would go through, I still subconsciously felt the need to keep my heart reserved.

I have heard a lot of people say that the moment it became real for them was when they heard the heartbeat for the first time. I went with Brianna and Jammie to one of her doctor appointments, and I heard that heartbeat. Still, even though I could see in the ultrasound that there was a baby in her belly, and I heard the little heart beating in that baby's chest, it still had not completely become real to me. I was still only *mostly* invested, not completely.

In the early days after Brianna contacted us, long before she came to Idaho, she had grown fond of the name Aiden James. James was the name of one of her relatives and Aiden was simply a name she liked. One day, as Jammie and I were talking, we decided to ask her if she would mind if we changed the middle name. We had grown accustomed to calling the baby Aiden, and we liked the name, but we also liked the idea of getting to be part of naming the child. We were nervous about asking her, but she said she was happy to go along with a change. For the time being, we decided on the middle name of Bryan, being that it is my father's name, and it was also similar to Brianna's name.

I was excited about that change. Still, it was only a day or two later that Jammie and I asked her if we could change the first name also. Her reaction was the same—she was happy to let us change it. Even though we were changing the name from what she had chosen, we had not yet picked out a new one. We wanted to do that together with her. We spent hours that evening making lists and comparing them.

My middle name is Ira. I got the name from my grandpa whom I admire and adore. Even though I had wanted to name my son Ira ever since I was a kid, I grew up thinking that my wife would not likely want to go along with it since it is such an uncommon name. Jammie had always told me she liked it, but I always wondered if she would change her mind when it actually came time to pick one. I thought it was even less likely that Brianna would like it, but after a few hours and after considering a few hundred names, the name Ira ended being chosen. I was surprised and elated.

Since the first name came from the top of my list, we thought it could be fun to choose the middle name from the top names on Brianna's list. Much to our surprise, the name

Porter was one of her favorite names. That name was high on all three of our lists. That was my great grandfather's name. That decision came pretty easily.

It is hard for me to explain why, but naming the child was a very big moment for me. Feeling the baby kick was nice, but it did not change much. Hearing the heartbeat and seeing the ultrasound was also nice, but it did not change a whole lot in me either. I found the line where, upon crossing it, I was fully invested. All my chips were in. There was no going back. If something went wrong in the process and this baby to be named Ira never came home with us, I would be utterly heart-broken. My defenses were now down.

Even though Brianna was committed to the adoption, and we were fully invested as well, the fact that we were sharing a home made it difficult to fully prepare ourselves for what was about to take place. We were on the receiving end of the adoption, and she was on the giving end. On the surface, it sounds like such a rosy and happy thing to think about, but it was not easy. We felt an incredible amount of guilt along with our joy. It was hard to not feel guilty for our happiness when someone else was going to have to suffer so much loss in order for us to get what we wanted—parenthood.

With every adoption, the expecting mother has to prepare for the difficulty of the great sacrifice she is about to make. It is physiologically and psychologically programmed into a woman's instincts to be difficult to say goodbye to her child, even if she knows it is the right thing to do. How was Brianna supposed to prepare herself for that? She did not know many people in Idaho other than us, and we were the ones on the other end of her difficult circumstance. Even though we loved her and she loved us, it was nearly impossible for us, the people she lived with, to be able to help her prepare for that sacrifice.

Also, Jammie and I needed to begin preparing our home for the baby's arrival. We needed things like baby clothes, a car seat, a baby swing and a crib. We wanted to prepare the baby's room for the new arrival, but the room that would become the nursery was being occupied by the young lady who was going to give birth to that baby.

We held off with as many of those preparations as possible in order to spare her feelings, but some preparations needed to be done sooner than later, and we had to do them right there in front of her. Whether the feelings were truly hers or whether they were just in our imagination, we felt guilty every time we sorted new baby clothes or bought home something new for the baby.

For all of the same reasons, we tried to keep our outward excitement to a minimum. We knew she wanted us to be excited, and we knew that she knew we were excited. Still, we felt guilty if we showed that too much in front of her, like we were rubbing it in her face.

Since we needed a little bit of time to prepare, and because she could use some space in order to prepare her heart for the separation, we discussed some new options with Brianna. We decided together on a day that she would begin staying with someone else. We felt that one week before her due date would be a good idea. This was a hard decision for us since we had grown accustomed to having her in our home. We also felt responsible for her. We were obviously invested and interested in every detail of her life. We enjoyed her company. We felt guilty for having her leave our home—like we were kicking her out—but we really needed the time to prepare emotionally and temporally.

The main reason we chose that time for her to stay with someone else was because that was when her mother would be arriving in Idaho to support her. She would not have to be left living alone with strangers.

We had a few options as to where the two of them could stay, and we let Brianna meet the families so she could choose. She chose Luke and Jill, some of our best friends who lived only a few blocks away. We made all of the preparations for Brianna and her mom to stay there. We thought we were all set.

Not many days before her mom arrived, however, Brianna expressed concern about how hard it would be to stay with Luke and Jill. They had three boys under the age of five, and being around that all day would be too much for her while trying to cope with her loss. All of the other families who had expressed a willingness to have them in their homes were in similar situations. Most of our close friends were our age, which meant that most of them had babies and toddlers.

Jammie and I drew up a new list of friends we trusted with a situation so delicate. This was a lot to ask of someone, and it was not easy to find a home with just a few days' notice. David and Joyce were friends from church who, after asking them if they could help, told us they needed to give it some thought. They ultimately agreed to take them in. They were exactly whom we were looking for since their kids were all grown up and moved out of the house. They had an available room in their house, and, above all, we trusted and admired them.

There was still a problem with the situation, though. David and Joyce were not going to be available to house them the entire time. Their spare room was only available *after* the baby was born, but not during the week prior to her due date.

Just two days before Brianna's mom was to arrive, we got a call from another friend, Marilyn, who told us she overheard Jammie and Joyce talking about our predicament at church. She and her husband, Joe, stepped into the role that we so desperately needed filled. Like David and Joyce, their children were all out of the home and they had a room. And also just like David and Joyce, we admired and trusted them fully.

We were all set.

When Brianna had hopped onto a plane a few months earlier, we had been worried about her flying standby and getting stuck in a strange airport somewhere. When it was her mother's turn to fly out west, we found that those worries had been justified. Her mother's flight plan was to make a few connection flights, ultimately arriving all the way to us at the Boise airport. She had a nightmare of a time trying to get her

61

seats on each connecting flight, and we were left in the dark wondering when she would arrive. She finally landed late at night, much later than we had originally expected her to arrive, but her luggage did not. It took a lot of work to sort it all out.

We dropped Brianna and her mother off at Joe and Marilyn's house before driving home. For the last time until some future day when our children would be grown up and gone, we were alone in our home with just our dogs to keep us company.

We had a lot to do to get ready during that week. Most of our needed preparations were mental. When Jammie and I needed a break, felt cooped up, or needed to talk about something, we took a walk together. We spent a lot of time over that last month wearing out the sidewalks around our neighborhood. Our walks became even more frequent the closer we came to the due date. We had a hard time talking about anything other than the upcoming adoption. In fact, on some of our walks we would tell ourselves that we were not allowed to talk about adoption, and we needed to find a different topic because of how much it consumed us.

Before Brianna's mother arrived to town, we were scared that the baby might be born before she came. Nobody wanted that to happen. Some Braxton Hicks contractions had us worried more than once that it might happen. Because her mom would have to get back to Mississippi for work, we also did not want Brianna to go past her due date. She had an appointment at 11:00 A.M. to be induced on her due date to ensure enough time to physically heal and be ready to return home when her mom needed to go back.

Jammie and I both had an impossible night's sleep ahead of us the night before her appointment. We made a weak attempt to go to bed early that night, knowing that we were in for a long day once we woke up. At 3:30 A.M., about two hours after I did finally fall asleep, my phone rang. The call was coming from Joe and Marilyn's house. It was time to wake up. It was time to jump in the car. It was time to pick them up. Brianna had gone into labor on her own a few hours before she was scheduled to be induced. It was time to drive to the hospital. It was time. It was time. It was time.

8

THE ROLLER COASTER RIDE

I had been to hospitals when some of my friends and family were having babies, but I had never been there for the whole show. I had always shown up near the end, waiting in the lobby or arriving after the baby was already born. Brianna was generous enough to let us be a part of her big day. Her mom was her most important supporter throughout the process, but we got to be the secondary comfort. She allowed us to be there in her room the entire time.

Jammie and I will never be able to thank Brianna enough for this. It would have been completely understandable, and we would have never dreamed of trying to change her mind if she preferred not to have us there. That time at the hospital belonged to her. The hospital room was hers. The day was hers. She chose to share it all with us.

She progressed quickly at first, which made me think the baby was coming right away. We had been looking forward to that moment for months, but now that it had arrived, I struggled to enjoy the moment because I was so tired. Back when I was a single college student, I used to work one or two graveyard shifts a week. With a few more years under my belt and a wedding ring on my finger, I had become accustomed to a steady sleeping schedule. I had become an incredible sissy when it came to losing sleep. Two hours of restless sleep was not enough.

I sat in my chair by Brianna's bedside trying to keep my eyes open while everyone else fulfilled their duties. I was relieved when the nurse gave her something to help with the pain, which slowed her labor down and eased her pains enough that Brianna fell asleep. The excitement mellowed, and about the time the sun came up, I was able to recline in my chair and take a nap. I slept for only about half an hour, but when I woke up I was a new man. I was ready.

Before that day, Jammie and I still hadn't had any direct contact with Brianna's father. We did not know how emotionally attached he was to the situation, but that became clear as the day unfolded. With Brianna obviously busy and distracted, Jammie kept him up-to-date with Brianna's progress. Text messages streamed constantly between their cell phones. His text responses were so quick that we pictured him pacing all morning with his phone in hand, waiting for every update. He sent a delivery man every few hours with flowers and other fun gifts to show he wished he could have been there. His presence and love were felt throughout the entire hospital experience, and it helped start a fun relationship with him that we have enjoyed ever since.

When time came for the big moment, everyone took their positions. Jammie and Brianna's mom stood on either side of the bed to give her emotional support. The doctor and the nurses stationed themselves at the foot of the bed for physical support. And I stood out of the way where I could cheer everyone else on.

Brianna was amazingly calm considering she had been in labor for over ten hours, and was delivering a baby for the first time. Jammie and Brianna stayed perfectly calm as well. I did my best to follow suit, but it did not take me long before I knew I would be wise to pull up a chair rather try to remain standing. The intensity of the situation was beginning to overwhelm me and I was starting to feel light-headed. My vision became cloudy as I came close to passing out, but I never did quite lose consciousness. I doubt Jammie will ever stop teasing me about that.

At about ten minutes before two o'clock in the afternoon, Brianna gave birth. As soon as I saw the tiny baby, I immediately looked wide-eyed at the doctor and nurses to see if their faces would show any alarm. I had seen babies that were a few minutes old before, but never one right when it was born, and I didn't know if a newborn was supposed to look like that. Everyone from the hospital staff appeared excited, so I breathed a sigh of relief knowing all was well.

The nurse handed me the scissors, and I tackled my only delivery room responsibility by cutting the cord.

The most beautiful little boy I had ever seen made his debut into our world. That's right—we now knew for sure that he was a boy.

Happy birthday to Ira Porter Elkins.

Ira, who happened to be born nine months after Jammie and I had first entered the adoption agency, was now part of our crazy world.

Jammie and I stood together, hand-in-hand, as we watched the nurses clean Ira up. When Jammie called out his name for the first time, he stopped crying for a moment and turned his head toward her. Many people might say it was just a coincidence, but it is much more fun to think it was not.

Something else interesting happened that day. My grandfather, the same grandpa who had the name Ira before me, was living in hospice care in another state at that time. On the same morning Ira was born, they hospice staff could not wake him up. The orderlies knew he was still alive, and they tried all of their normal tricks to awaken him, but he never did the entire day. The next day he woke up and, as if nothing out of the ordinary had happened, told the orderly he was hungry.

I like to think Granddad was there in our hospital room with us that day. He will always be someone very special to me, and I like to think he got to take a short vacation from his frail body—even if it was just for a day—to come spend some time with us. I like to think that the love of his life, my grandmother, who had passed away a few years before, came to take him on his little vacation and that they got to watch the whole thing unfold from the other side. I like to think it was not a coincidence that the day he did not wake up was the same day his great grandson, who received his name, was born.

***

As I said before, the stay at the hospital belonged to Brianna. We, ourselves, were guests there. This baby was not ours. He was still Brianna's baby. Although the hospital gave Jammie and me our own room separate from Brianna's, it was still Brianna's situation. It was hard for some of our friends to understand, but we did not feel like it was our place to invite a lot of friends and family to come share in the joy. Plus, it was a deeply emotional time for everyone, and it was nice to share it mainly with just Brianna and her mom.

That being said, with Brianna's approval, we did invite a select few to come visit the hospital. My mother was in town to help out with anything we might need as well as help with my brother's family since they were expecting a baby on the same day. My sister-in-law, Beth, did not go into labor that day, so she and Clark came with my mom to see us. We knew their kids were excited to meet their new cousin, but the time was not right, and we asked them to wait until Ira could come home with us before meeting him.

Although Ira spent the majority of that afternoon and evening with us in our room, we knew it was always Brianna's right to see Ira whenever she wished. If she asked for him, we did not hesitate to bring him to her. It was not easy. We fell in love with him from the first second we laid our eyes on him, and we were terrified something might happen to take Ira away from us. Mainly, we were scared about their bonding time. We were scared she might bond too closely to him, and she would not be able to put her signature on the release papers. We were afraid her emotions might take over, and she would not be able to let him go.

Jammie felt a strong impression to ask Brianna if she wanted to spend some time with Ira before going to bed that first night, and Brianna said she would. We brought little Ira into her room, and left them alone. We told her to let us know when she wanted us to come back since the plan was for him to spend the night with us in our room.

We did not set a time for our return to her room, so we did not know how long she would want to spend with him. Judging by how long she chose to hold him throughout the day, we expected her to want to snuggle him for ten or fifteen minutes.

We waited.

Fifteen minutes passed and we still had not heard from them. We tried to find something on TV worth watching, but nothing could take our minds off the situation, so we just turned it off.

Thirty minutes passed. I have a hard time sitting still when I am nervous, so I paced around the floor. What was going on in the other room?

Forty-five minutes passed and our minds started racing through different scenarios of what they might be thinking or doing in their room. Why had she not called for us to come pick him up?

Sixty minutes passed and we were starting to go out of our minds. Was something the matter? How closely were they bonding? We got out some playing cards and began playing the slowest game of SKIP-BO in history. Was she going to keep Ira all night?

Seventy-five minutes passed and time felt like it was moving as slowly as our card game. What frame of mind was Brianna in? Was she going to be able to sign the custody papers in the morning?

Ninety minutes passed and we just could not handle the suspense anymore. Even if she told us she needed more time, we just had to know. Our minds felt flooded with possibilities and we were drowning.

We knocked softly, and poked our heads into her room. The first thing we saw was Brianna's red puffy eyes. She had been crying. We did not know what to say or what to ask, but once we started talking, it did not take long before we were reassured that everything was okay. The issue that had made her cry had nothing to do with Ira or adoption. She and her mom were working through something completely separate.

They had been caught up in conversation, not realizing how scared we were in the other room. We shared some hugs with them before retiring to our room for the night with Ira. We left on a happy note. What a relief!

Jammie took care of Ira most of the night. We had agreed to take turns waking up to feed Ira, but she let me sleep through most of my turns until she was finally too tired.

As long as Brianna needed to stay in the hospital for her recovery, Ira needed to stay there too, even though he was usually with us down the hall. Since we had some extra time, we thought it could be fun to make the best of it by having a birthday party. We asked a friend to bring a cake, and Brianna's dad sent another basket of treats, which we ate together with the nurses to celebrate Ira's birthday. Brianna was feeling in good spirits. We still felt nervous when Brianna spent time bonding with Ira, but not as much as the previous day.

The next morning, a little more than 48 hours after we had arrived at the hospital, the hard part came. It was time to leave. Jon, along with the hospital caseworker, spent a lot of time going over the paperwork. We were not present in Brianna's room during any of their conversations, but we knew emotions were more elevated than they had been at any other time. Putting her signature on the line was difficult for her, but that is her story to tell, not mine. Suffice it to say that even though we had a fun evening with her the night before, we were still really nervous about whether or not she would go through with it.

She was strong. She followed through with her plan, even though it was difficult. She signed the papers.

Even with that done, we were still far from everything being final. The papers she signed that morning were only to release temporary custody to the adoption agency. The agency, in turn, assigned us to care for the child. Custody still belonged to Brianna and Daren until the time would come for Brianna to stand in front of a judge, which we expected to take place in about a week. After Brianna's time in front of a judge, it would still take another few months before Jammie and I could finalize everything through the court system.

There were still a lot of hoops to jump through, which kept us scared that something might go wrong. We had Baby Ira with us now, and we were madly in love with him, but we were terrified something might happen to take that away from us.

Those fears would only intensify over the coming weeks as we found ourselves at the mercy of more difficulties.

9

FRANTIC FIRST DAYS

Open adoption comes with interesting internal battles that can sometimes take a long time to resolve. Are we parents or are we permanent babysitters? We can easily tell ourselves that we, of course, are parents, but sometimes what we know and the way we feel do not match.

Ira was now in our home, but we still did not have anything signed by a judge declaring us to be parents. Brianna still had legal say over Ira, and temporary custody still belonged to the adoption agency—not to us. Even though we were the ones waking up at all hours of the night to warm up a bottle and change a diaper, we did not have any more legal rights to Ira than any stranger walking down the street. At that time we were still babysitters hoping to become parents, even though we loved him as if he were already our son.

Meanwhile, Brianna and her mom were staying with David and Joyce. We stressed and worried about Brianna. How much was she struggling now that the little boy who had been inside her for the last nine months was now with us a few blocks away? Was she regretting her decision? She was still about a week away from her court appearance. Was she going to change her mind?

All of the stresses and insecurities intensified when she and her mom arrived on our doorstep for a visit the next day. We could see by the look on her face the moment she arrived on our doorstep that she had been struggling mightily. We tried to have a nice visit, but she was full of a million questions and she voiced them all one by one.

What if one of us died? What if both of us died? What if we divorced? Were we going to turn our backs on her now that we had Ira? All of her questions were justified, and all of her concerns were legitimate, but there was not much we could say. Nobody can promise he or she will not die, and people do not get married expecting to divorce. All we could really do was assure her that our marriage was strong, our hobbies and interests were not life-threatening, and we loved her too much to ever cut her off.

The thought of asking anything at all from Brianna at such a delicate time made us uncomfortable, but we felt like we needed to. For our own sake as well as for hers, we needed to plan some sort of schedule so we could know how often to expect visits while they were still in Idaho.

I have felt God's guidance a number of times in my life, but there have been only a few times when I've said something that literally felt like it came from someone else. This was one of those times.

"We are going to let you make that decision yourself, Brianna," I said. "Don't make it here. Not right now. After you go back to David and Joyce's, take a moment to ponder how often you want to come over while you're still in Idaho. The decision is completely yours to make. If you want to visit every day, we'll make that happen. If you don't want to come at all anymore, that's fine too. You can decide how often, and you can decide for how long you want each visit to be. It's up to you."

I was surprised when those words came out of my mouth. I had not previously considered the idea of giving Brianna complete control over visits like this, especially not now that she was such an emotional mess. I had not discussed this with Jammie either, but I knew it was right for our situation as soon as those words came out of my mouth.

Brianna nodded her head in agreement then turned her eyes back to Ira, whom she was holding swaddled in her arms.

"I don't know if I can let you go," Brianna said as she continued to cry. "I don't know if I can. I don't know if I can."

When Brianna left, she was a wreck. We were a wreck. Our emotions were so paper thin that we felt like we were being blown all over the place. We called Jon and we called the lady who ran the support group for birthmothers. They helped calm our nerves whenever we called, but over the next two days our worries were never more than a millimeter from our minds. Was she regretting her decision? Was she going to change her mind? Could she let him go?

Brianna's mother was in an interesting position. She was watching her daughter struggle, and yet she knew she had to leave the final decision up to Brianna. At the same time she made sure to tell us on many occasions that we should not worry. She told us that even though Brianna was going through a really rough time she was confident Brianna was not going to go back on her decision.

When Brianna and her mother were back at David and Joyce's place that evening, they talked over a schedule. They decided to come every other day until they left town. Each visit was going to be an hour long. That seemed like a good plan to us. It felt good to have something for which we could plan.

The next visit was very different from the first. This time, Brianna came through our front door with a huge smile on her face. When she held Ira, she focused more on enjoying his presence rather than dreading the thought of giving him away. Indeed, as we've heard many people in the adoption world say, she seemed to understand better that she was not giving him up, but that she was giving him more.

Before they came, we did not have any reason to think the second visit would be different from the first, so we were really nervous—maybe even more so than before the first visit. Not only did her demeanor make us feel more comfortable this time, but we able to enjoy seeing the two of them together. And when she purposefully referred to Ira as "Russ and Jammie's baby," we could not help but love her even more. I know that may not seem like a lot to some people, but it meant the world to us. It helped us feel legitimate in the role we were playing. Even though we were still legally just babysitters, she made us feel like much more.

A few weeks later, with the gift of hindsight, we were able to fully understand why it was important for Brianna to be allowed to set her own schedule. It helped her feel like she had some say in what was going on. It would have been harder for her to cope with the situation if she was not allowed to have any control. And by waiting until she was back at David and Joyce's place—a neutral environment—she was able to think more with her rational mind, and not just with her emotions. During her subsequent visits, she did not have such a hard time handing Ira back over to us because she knew what time she would be leaving, and when she would be coming back.

Everybody's emotions were still up and down all week. Just the simple fact that we were brand new parents was enough to make our emotions ebb and flow, and adding the drama of our situation made it even more so.

Our questions and concerns about whether or not Brianna would sign the court papers were never completely out of our minds, but our visits were going well, and each time she came to our home we felt more confident that she would sign. By the time her court date came, a week after leaving the hospital, we felt pretty secure.

Jammie and I did not go with Brianna and Jon to court, and neither did Ira. We waited at home by the phone. They brought with them all of the correspondence Brianna had with Daren over the previous months to show he was not interested in being a father, and that she was not hiding or lying about her situation. To my understanding, the judge did not hesitate and Brianna stayed firm in her decision, although I am sure it was not easy for her.

Our phone rang right about the time we were expecting it to, and we knew we had just cleared another hurdle. Brianna's decision to place her baby for adoption was now permanent. Brianna and Daren both had no more legal rights to Ira than any other person walking down the street. Of course, we didn't either. The soonest we could hope for a court date was still a few months away. Now that Brianna's day in court was done, we still had two last things on our to-do list before she and her mom headed back south. The first of those was a photo session.

Jammie, being a photographer, got one of her photographer friends to take the pictures for us in her home studio. We had a lot of fun, and got some great shots despite the fact that Ira was in a wiggly mood. We will cherish those pictures forever.

The second thing on our checklist was to have a sweet sixteen birthday party for her since her birthday fell just before her departure day. We made her wear a funny newspaper hat, which matched one we made for Ira, and sang the birthday song purposefully off tune. She opened some gifts and we ate some cake with the people she grew close to while being with us. We did not expect David to make it to the party since he had to work, but he found a way to come.

Everything appeared to be done—at least for the time being. Brianna's court papers had been filed. We had finished our photo shoot. We had celebrated her sixteenth birthday. She had wrapped up all the loose ends, and when morning came the next day, she was ready to go. It made us feel good to see how much she looked forward to seeing her family and friends back in Mississippi. She had not seen them for over two months, and she missed them all. The most important thing about it was seeing her focus change to what was in front of her rather than stay focused on the baby that she was leaving behind.

With all of these things accomplished, we felt like the next few months would consist of mostly technicalities before we could coast to the finish line to finalize the adoption. Those assumptions were proven to be wrong when Ira's birthfather and his family decided enter into the picture again.

10

THE STORM BEFORE THE CALM

Our new life had begun. Sure, we were not legally parents yet, but we were on the home stretch. We still had a lot of growing to do together, but our relationship with Brianna was blossoming. We thought we could just coast to the finish line—where an Idaho state judge would be waiting with her gavel and maybe even a handful of helium-filled balloons. That was not at all how it happened, though.

We decided to contact Daren. It had been a while since he and Brianna had contact, so it seemed like a good time. We wanted him to be included in Ira's life if he wanted to be.

We wrote to him a short e-mail message. We not only told him we were willing to send pictures and information, but we were interested in knowing more about him so we could answer Ira's questions once he was older. We didn't just tell him we were okay with having contact with him—we tried to encourage it. That being said, it was not going to come without any effort on his part. We wanted just two simple things from him. First, as long as Brianna wanted to be left alone, he would have to honor her wish. Second, he had to respond to our e-mail and tell us that he *did* want pictures and updates. We were not going to send pictures and letters without knowing for sure that was what he wanted.

We did not know if he would even respond. And if he did, we did not know if he would write an angry or a nice letter. He did not respond to us by e-mail at all, but he did take that as his cue to contact and pester Brianna some more. That was not the response we were hoping for.

A few more weeks passed, and through the grapevine Brianna found out Daren was taking pictures of Ira off of our Facebook pages. We had not realized someone could do that without our permission, so we quickly figured out how to change our security settings.

Some people might ask why we would block him from access to our pictures, while also offering to send him pictures. It is simple. Ira, just because of the fact that he is adopted, is already going to have enough drama in his life. He does not need any extra. We did not like the idea of someone sidestepping us to have contact with our little boy.

Soon after that, Jammie got two requests from girls who wanted to become her Facebook friends. Many people automatically accept new friend requests even if they do not know who it is from, but not us. Jammie wrote them both back, asking how she knew them. One of them responded, saying she mistook Jammie for someone else. Before the second one could respond, Jammie dug around and discovered that both of them were Daren's cousins.

Jammie wrote the second cousin again, told her that she knew who she was, and asked what she was hoping for by requesting access to her page. She and Jammie exchanged three or four e-mails, all of which showed that she was very understanding of our situation as well as feeling sympathetic to her cousin, Daren. She seemed like a nice person. Her petition to become Jammie's Facebook friend, however, was denied. She understood when Jammie told her we would be happy for her to have pictures, but we wanted Daren to be the key to opening the communication door with his family and friends. She had our e-mail. She knew how we could easily be contacted. And just in case Daren somehow did not get the e-mail we sent before, we asked her to request of him the same two things we contacted him about. Still, Daren gave no response to us, and he continued to bother Brianna.

What happened next terrified us.

Brianna was quietly minding her own business, busily working at her new job in a pizzeria, when someone showed up with court papers. She called us immediately after she got off work, and read us the papers which made it clear that Daren was planning to use the courts to take Ira away from us.

Jammie and I had grown more in love with our little Ira every second of every day. Was all that going to be shattered? Were we going to lose him?

We had not seen this coming, and we were now more terrified than ever before.

If Jon had any minutes left on his cell phone, I am sure we exhausted every last one of them and more between the time we heard about the court summons and the day Brianna was to appear in court. He continued to do his best to assure us we had done everything ethically and legally, but there was no consoling us this time. We were a wreck.

We could not leave the situation alone, wanting updates from Brianna or Jon any chance we could get. It was hard to get information because Brianna and Jon were both getting their information through secondhand or thirdhand sources themselves. Every day dragged on and no news ever brought us comfort.

During all of this, Ira was still in the legal custody of the adoption agency, which was both a negative and a positive. It was negative because we knew my wife and I had no legal rights to this child we loved with all our hearts. It was positive because the agency had an amazing team of lawyers throughout the country who were taking care of the situation. We would have struggled to afford the help of an attorney since this adoption process had already run our bank accounts dry. There was not much we could do other than pray. Boy, we sure did our fair share of praying—as did all of our friends close to us.

We could not figure out why Daren suddenly cared enough to seek custody after so many months of zero interest from him. It would have been much easier for him to make this decision to parent *before* Ira was born, rather than wait until after his rights had already been terminated. I figured he must not have taken Brianna seriously when she told him what her plan was. That was the only thing that made sense to me.

Then we found out that the real reason was because he had never actually told his parents that Brianna was having a baby. They did not even know! Since Brianna and Daren had broken up, he did not bother to tell them otherwise. I do not even know his reasons for doing so, but he somehow kept it a secret from them until Brianna returned to Mississippi and word got to his mom. From the secondhand information we received, it was clear that the driving force behind all the recent activity was Daren's mom, not Daren.

Brianna's court date was marked on our calendar, and we nervously watched the day inch closer and closer. There was no escaping it. It was coming and we were helpless to stop it. The lawyers kept assuring us that we had done everything right.

We bit our fingernails and watched the phone all day until Jon finally called. It was over. It was done. Ira was going to stay in our home. What a relief!

We had been kept mostly in the dark about the details until afterward, but it turned out that the agency's lawyer worked alongside the caseworker to solve the issue outside of court. At the last minute, the wrinkles in the situation were ironed out without Brianna or anyone else needing to set foot in any courtroom.

I breathed a huge sigh of relief that day, but I have never been able to look back on it with a smile. In a perfect world, Daren and Brianna would both be an active part in Ira's open adoption. The dispute only lasted a couple of weeks, but it has always brought me pain to think of battling with Daren over custody.

When I think about it, I see Brianna wanting *us* to raise Ira, and Daren wanting his *mother* to raise him. Neither Brianna nor Daren were ready or interested in raising him, and only they had the right to decide who would do so. Jammie and I had no right to say he belonged to us. Brianna's aunt and uncle who said he should come to them because they were family had no right to him. Daren's mother had no more claim on Ira than anyone other than Daren or Brianna. Since Daren and Brianna would never agree on who should raise Ira, and since he never offered even the tiniest amount of emotional or financial support during her pregnancy, it seemed reasonable to me that Brianna should be the one to make that decision.

Plus, Brianna told us over and over that there was no way she would allow Ira to be raised in that home. If they were to have succeeded in reversing the judge's decision, then Ira would have returned to Brianna's arms, and she would have raised Ira herself. She would have dropped out of school, abandoned her hopes of becoming a nurse, and spent her time at home as a single teenage mother.

Daren and his parents did not pursue the matter any further. All of the really scary stuff went away, but the childish games were still there. We reached out to Daren one more time, now that all of the ugly court stuff was finished, to see if he was interested in our previous offer. His response was pretty much the same, choosing to ignore our e-mail and hassling Brianna some more.

This time he got one of Brianna's closest friends in on it. I do not know if it was Daren's idea or if she did it on her own, but she started taking pictures of Ira from Jammie's Facebook page, and giving them to him. We had been very careful about which Mississippi friends to allow access to our Facebook pages, and since Jammie and this particular friend had bonded over some heart-to-heart conversations, we did not think it would be a problem. We were wrong. With access to Jammie's account, she was copying pictures and giving them to Daren. How frustrating. We had already reached out to him twice directly and once indirectly through his cousin. We felt like we had done everything but show up on his doorstep or talk to his mom just to try to get him to agree, but he kept playing games.

We'd had enough of the drama. We apologized to everyone we had to block from our Facebook accounts, and deleted all of the Mississippi contacts except for Brianna's immediate family. We did not write Daren anymore.

11

FINALLY FINAL

There was no way of knowing how long we might have to wait for our own day in court to finalize the adoption. When our lawyer called to tell us something opened up, and asked if we wanted it, we jumped at the chance. It had been a while since one of our "surprises" had been a good one, so this was a nice change. The thought of the adoption being legitimate and final had us bubbling with excitement.

Even though we wanted to shout our excitement to the whole world, we did not need or want the whole world to show up to the courtroom. Court was held on a weekday during work hours, so we only invited a very small handful of people. That was enough for us.

I had not been in a courtroom since I was a teenager who had been caught speeding. I was a little intimidated by the big oak stand, the judge sitting above us, an air of seriousness hanging over everything, and a bunch of fancy courtroom talk. However, we were not worried about a thing. Our attorney could take care of that awkward legal stuff.

The judge talked sternly about the seriousness of what we were about to undertake. She found it important to repeatedly drive home the point that we were not going to be able to return the child if we decided later that parenthood was not our thing.

After a sufficient amount of sober and serious talk, her lips curled up into a smile. She did not bang her gavel, but she simply said, "It is done." Just like that, it was official. Leaving that courtroom did not give us any new responsibilities we did not already have, but we were officially not babysitters anymore. We were parents! Ira was now part of our forever family.

When we got back to our little home I told Jammie I felt like we just ran a marathon. It felt so good to be where we now were, but the whole process was so exhausting that I did not know how long it would take before I could say I was ready to adopt again.

This race was over, but we knew we could not stop moving. This adoption was an open adoption, so we would still have obligations to fulfill for many years to come.

We made a lot of promises to Brianna going into the adoption, and we had every intention of keeping them. We did not really know what we were getting ourselves into when we made those promises. We had taken classes and read about others' experiences, but open adoption is one of those things we could have never truly understood until we lived it. Besides, even if we had lived it before, every adoption is different.

Brianna pulled away from us a little in order to move on with her life. We still talked on the phone and exchanged e-mails, but not as often as before. Oftentimes we were anxious to know how she was doing, but we did not want to pry when she needed space. Even when we were not conversing a lot, adoption still consumed our minds.

Sharing pictures turned out to be a greater responsibility than we had anticipated and it was difficult to know how to go about it. We had not discussed with Brianna how often we would post pictures, supposing we could figure it out as we went along. When we questioned other birthmothers, they each had different ideas about how often we should share them. Some birthmothers made it sound like too many pictures made it hard for them to move on with their life. Other birth-mothers made it sound like too few pictures made them feel abandoned. Most birthmothers made it sound like their needs kept changing over time, wanting a lot of photos one month, and then nothing the next.

When we thought about pictures before Ira was born, we thought the main difficulty would be the time it would take to share them. After he was born, however, we discovered that only covered part of the difficulty. Adoption is emotion-ally consuming. Both before and long after Ira was born, our emotions bounced all over the place. We felt the joy of finally having that perfect little baby in our home, but we also felt the guilt that Brianna was going through something difficult to bring us that joy. It tore us apart to think of her suffering.

Posting pictures did take time, but that was nothing compared to the stress adoption already had on us. Even many months later, we still thought about it all day, every day. Oftentimes we found ourselves just wanting a mental break from having to think about it so much. The stress around posting updates was mostly because it intensified the fixation our minds already had on the subject of adoption—much more than the time it took to do it.

On the other hand, we truly did want to share the pictures with Brianna and her family. We started to form a fun relationship with some of her family members whom we had never met face-to-face. We enjoyed sharing Ira's photos with them, and we loved hearing back from them when they sent comments about the photos. Jammie set up a special blog with a password just for Brianna, separate from our own family blog, so Brianna could check it whenever she wanted.

Another reason pictures and updates proved to be harder than we anticipated was because we did not enjoy feeling as if we were babysitters anymore. Even though we understood and respected Brianna's role in the situation, Ira was our little boy. Having the responsibility of giving someone updates and photos made us feel like we had to check in with her. Feeling like we had to report to someone else made us feel like we were not the ultimate authority when it came to our little Ira. And if we felt like we were not the ultimate authority, did that mean someone else must be the parent? Our rational minds told us that we were indeed parents, but our emotional minds played tug-of-war with those feelings.

Once we started realizing what feelings and emotions accompanied the responsibility of an open adoption, we could somewhat understand why some adoptive parents cut off communication from the birthparents. We could see it, but that did not mean we accepted it. If contact with Brianna got to a point where we decided it was unhealthy for Ira to continue, we would obviously have made serious changes, but we had made her promises and we intended to keep them. Even though the photos and updates weighed heavily on us at times, we loved Brianna. We loved her then and we always will, so even during the times when our emotions were most intense, cutting her off was not an option.

The difficulty we felt with the updates and photos was all on our side. It was all in our own minds. What I mean is, Brianna was not saying or doing things to make us feel like she questioned our role. There were a couple of times when she asked for certain pictures, but she was never overly demanding or needy. When we felt like the situation was keeping us from feeling like we were Ira's parents, it was because we were facing something that we, ourselves, needed to overcome. Brianna was on our side—not against us. And although we knew this, accepting it was still easier said than done.

Finally, when it came to choosing photos, we struggled to know how many and how often were the correct amount. Everybody we knew had an opinion, of course, but they were not part of our situation. Even other adoptive couples and other birthparent could not fully understand our situation because the chemistry between Brianna and us was different than it was for other adoptive families.

95

There were times when we wondered if we were posting too often on the blog. We could tell she was dying to see them, but at the same time we wondered if having them so readily available kept her from being able to progress. We tried hard to read her state of mind, but reading single-line statements on her Facebook page was rarely enough of a window into her mind to really know what to think. We avoided asking ourselves the question, "Is it really our responsibility to know how she's doing?" We felt responsible for her happiness because we were the beneficiaries of what was paining her. We felt responsible for her ability to move on because we felt guilty about wanting to progress ourselves. We felt responsible for her well-being because she sacrificed so much for us. Our rational minds would say that we needed to give her some space so that those people closest to her could help her heal, but our emotional minds still played tug-of-war with it.

Through the passing months we noticed that our ability to heal and progress was paralleled with how we envisioned Brianna's progress. We felt more calm and at ease with our role when we felt like she was happy. We felt more guilty than usual if we thought she was struggling, even when her struggles were not related to adoption. I know it was probably unhealthy to mirror someone else's state like that, but that was how it was for a long time.

12

A VISIT FROM A FAMILIAR FACE

We had chosen to open our lives to Brianna so she could watch Ira grow, and also so that Ira could know his biological roots. Having our adoption be so open was not easy, and we never felt that more than while we planned for Brianna's first return visit. She was coming back to Idaho!

On a number of occasions, we tried to make arrangements for her to come, but plans fell through every time. When she first left Idaho to return home, our plan was for her to visit sometime that summer, which would have been about six months later. We were all really excited about it. As the months went by, and as Brianna felt farther and farther away, our excitement changed to worry. We became more protective of our title as "parents," and anything that could jeopardize that title made us uncomfortable. It was probably a good thing our summer visit fell through because I am not so sure we were mentally ready for it yet.

We considered having her come for Thanksgiving, but that fell through. We talked about having her come for Ira's first birthday, but the timing would have been bad for her schooling. The idea of spring break came up but that was soon forgotten as well. We knew we would do it someday, but two thousand miles between us made it difficult for her to just drop by.

Then one day Brianna's sister called us wondering about our Christmas break plans. She was planning a trip to Salt Lake City to visit some friends, and wanted to bring Brianna along as a Christmas gift. She asked if they could make the five hour drive to Boise while they were in the Mountain West area.

The scenario was perfect. All of the previous plans we made, which had all fallen through, were plans made months before the visit would take place, and all those plans included her staying for about a week. With this short notice, being only a couple of weeks away, we did not have as much time to fret and stress. And since their drive to Boise was only going to be a small part of their vacation, they planned on staying for just twenty-four hours. The thought of having them in our home for longer than a day was not something we were necessarily scared of, but we had so many questions surrounding the visit that a shortened stay sounded ideal for the first one.

After Ira was born, and Brianna returned to Mississippi, I had said to Jammie a week later that I missed having her in our home. We had grown accustomed to having her with us, and we loved her as part of our family. Being almost a year later, though, her memory now felt distant. The distance and the time apart added up to uncertainty. We still loved her like we did when she lived in our home, but we were used to having our home to ourselves again. We were nervous about what might transpire when she came back to visit.

How would we feel if she called herself Ira's mom? We did not want a tug-of-war over who could claim parenthood. What if Ira seemed more attached to her than to us while she was around? We did not want to feel unimportant. What if being back in our home stirred up difficult emotions for her? We had struggled with our own feelings of guilt for so long that we worried watching her struggle might set us back. Our minds flooded with questions.

The day came, and she was on her way. We were excited and at the same time very nervous. When their rental car pulled up to our house, we ran out to greet them. She was now back in our home and it did not take long before our fears dissipated.

Not only did she seem aware of our insecurities, but she went out of her way to show us that she sustained us as Ira's parents. In fact, she repeatedly referred to us as such, calling us his mom and dad when she was talking to Ira, which meant more to us than anything else she could have done. She talked about positive things, and she made us feel like she approved of the way we were parenting him. That meant the world to us as well. It helped us relax. It helped us take a step back from our emotions to look at the bigger picture where we saw Brianna just wanting to be allowed to love Ira. She was not trying to take anything away from us, and she did a great job of helping us to see that.

Having her back in our home brought back wonderful feelings that had been hiding behind our insecurities. We had not forgotten about our love for her, but memories were not the same as having her physically present again. Once she was with us, and she showed us that she was not a threat, we found that we were more than willing to let her back into our circle. We were happy to let her hold him. We were happy to let them play together on the floor. We were happy to let them interact. We were happy to let them bond. It was a wonderful feeling to be able to enjoy watching them together.

Their visit was short. Many of our friends knew she was coming, and they all wanted an update afterward. It was fun to say "better than we could have imagined" when telling them the details of how it went.

Some of our friends told us they thought the visit would be a bad idea. Those same friends constantly told us it would be bad for our family if we kept the adoption open, but they were not in our shoes, and they did not understand our situation the way we did. We knew ourselves, and we knew this was right for us. Open adoption can be very intimidating and scary, but we do not wish we had it any other way. We keep our adoption promises because we love the relationship it has built.

A funny thing happened after Brianna left to go home again. Her acceptance and support of our parenthood meant so much to us that everything inside of our hearts regarding adoption relaxed. It changed the way our minds processed the situation. We now look forward to a second visit someday rather than being scared like we were of the first one. Sending her pictures feels different now too. Having confidence that she sustains us helps us feel more like we were *sharing* the pictures rather than feeling like we were *reporting* to someone. In fact, oftentimes when we take some fun pictures, Brianna is the first one we think of and we cannot wait to share them with her.

We have not spent a lot of time talking about it with her, but we have felt things change on her end as well. It has been comforting for us to watch her heal and pull away enough to live her teenage life again. We had not been able to separate our emotions from hers during that first year while she struggled because we mirrored her emotional state, so it was nice to be able to watch her heal. She had already been progressing before the visit, but the visit seemed to serve as a catalyst to push that forward even more.

We make a good partnership—Brianna and us. We strongly feel she made the right decision when she chose us as a couple. I am not boasting that Jammie and I are the most extraordinary couple, but I mean we are good for each other. Brianna is good for us, and we are good for Brianna. We love her, and she loves us. We make a good partnership.

13

OPEN ABOUT ADOPTION

With each passing month, Ira became more and more "ours." Of course, we will never forget the sacrifice Brianna made to bring him to us, but the way we looked at him became different. When he was brand new it seemed like every time I held him in my arms I thought about the process of how he came to be there. With time, though, I did not think about those things as much. I just looked at him and saw him for who he was. I saw him as my son.

It is always funny when other people forget he was adopted, especially those closest to us. Even my own mother said once, "Ya know, he doesn't really look like his cousins." Jammie looked at her wondering if she was joking, or if she had actually forgotten for a second that he had a completely different set of genes than any of his cousins. She had forgotten. It was funny, and at the same time it was refreshing. It is nice to feel that other people see him primarily as our son and do not think about the adoption first. Even Brianna's mother said something to us once, forgetting for a second that Ira had come to us through her own daughter. Some things make me laugh no matter how often they happen.

Even when they mean well, people sometimes say things that can really hit a soft spot inside of us. The struggle against feeling like we were Ira's permanent babysitters was probably our greatest hurdle. Since people in the general public do not typically use the same terminology we do, sometimes what they *try* to say does not come out like we want to hear it. For example, many people do not know to use the terms "birthmom" or "biological mother." They only know one word—mom. And since a lot of people met Brianna while she was living with us, it is natural for them to wonder how she is doing. People sometimes ask us how Ira's mom is doing. To us, Jammie is "Mom." Oftentimes I will answer that by saying, "Oh, Jammie is fine," usually for my own humor's sake, and other times I respond by saying "*Brianna,* his birthmother, is doing well," emphasizing her name.

One lady commented on how much Ira loved music, and she said his mom must really enjoy music. That one poked me a little extra hard because, on top of the fact that she referred to Brianna as his mom, it undermined the nurturing part of child development. In my strong opinion, a large part of the reason Ira loves music so much is because I have played the guitar for him almost every day of his life. Plus, Jammie and I sing to him every night as we put him to bed. I am not saying that his nature and genetics do not contribute to who he is, because they certainly do, but it is never fun to have people disregard our role in Ira's life.

Many people really do get it, though. Sure, those who say hurtful or insensitive things stand out in our minds, but the truth is they're in the minority. It can feel like it is more common than it is because hurtful words weigh more than positive words, especially since adoption is so important to us.

I realized one day that I was also not perfect at thinking before I talk. I do not always consider other people when words spill out of my mouth.

I was talking to a good friend and venting some frustration about something someone had said. At that time, he had one daughter and she was not adopted, so I continued talking and talking as if he was not able to relate. He sat quietly and listened to everything I said. When he did finally say something, he spoke as if he could relate. I brushed it off and continued talking. When he commented a second time, I realized and remembered that his daughter is his stepdaughter. I do not know his wife's ex-husband, so I never think of his daughter as his stepdaughter.

My mind never made the connection that he was in a similar situation to us. Actually, if I was in his shoes, I would probably struggle even more because of how his wife's ex-husband would go out of his way to remind him just who the little girl's biological father was. My friend never said anything to make me feel like I was insensitive, but I left the conversation realizing that I need to cut people more slack when they're insensitive.

Sometimes people misunderstandings can be humorous. When we were shopping for a car seat before Ira was born, the sales lady asked us how soon the baby was due. We told her we were expecting him in just three days, and her eyes shot immediately to Jammie's midsection. Jammie and I both have a similar sense of humor, so neither of us explained her lack of a belly until she stewed over it for ten seconds. We got a good laugh out of it. She was probably thinking we might be wise to go get ourselves an ultrasound before we made too many purchases.

After Ira was born, we enjoyed everybody's reaction when they asked how old he was. Women would usually respond by saying they wished their body bounced back as quickly as Jammie's did. Some things are funny every time.

Conversations with strangers almost always started that way. They would ask how old Ira was, and then comment on how quickly Jammie lost her baby weight. Next, the conversation would inevitably slide right into adoption. If we were going out into the public we could count on adding twenty minutes to every trip because adoption almost always comes up. We enjoyed it. There would have been easy ways to avoid the conversation if we wanted to, but we were both so proud of adoption that we never shied away from talking about it.

Our positive view of adoption was the main reason we liked to talk about it so much, but we also wanted to stand as advocates for the cause because we had not known just how much opposition there was to adoption. We met people who spoke out against adoption because they did not feel like adopted children were as loved by their parents as children who were not adopted. Many people feel that children should always be raised by family, never by strangers. Some feel that the *only* responsible thing for an unplanned pregnancy is to get married and raise the child.

Some people see infant adoption as stealing babies. I've even been called an "adoptaraptor," which made me laugh. I'm sorry, but if you're trying to insult me, I am not going to feel bad if you use cutesy words like that. They picture people like us and adoption agencies as those who stalk birthmothers and pressure them into doing something they do not want to do.

The list of reasons people oppose adoption goes on and on, all of which became very apparent to us after we adopted. We now know that the world needs more people speaking up in favor of it.

The trends regarding adoption have changed over the last handful of decades, leading to where we are now with far fewer adoptions than in the past. There are consistently about ten abortions performed for every adoption that takes place in the United States. Grandmothers are more willing now to take custody of their grandchildren. It is more socially acceptable now for teenagers to have babies and become mothers. Being a single mother, no matter her age, is much more common and more accepted in society than in the past. Government welfare programs help support low-income households, which can be a big factor if the father is not there for support.

I, personally, have a real problem with the concept of elective abortion. All of the other trends that I just mentioned, though, are not necessarily a bad thing. I have a lot of friends who are either single parents or grew up in a single-parent home, and their home life is beautiful. Sometimes Grandma is the perfect choice for raising a child. Jammie and I know a lot of teenage mothers who have chosen to raise their babies, and we have no hesitation in saying their decision to parent was right for their situation.

I was shocked when I started to see the pressure that a single mother is put under after others find out she's pregnant. I am not specifically talking about Brianna here, though she did feel it too. There's an incredible amount of pressure from family members for a single mother to keep the baby, sometimes saying that she dug herself into a hole, and the only responsible thing to do would be to take care of it. Other family might pressure her into keeping the baby because they want to be a grandma, or uncle, or whatever. The bottom line is that outside pressures from peripheral people sometimes push an expecting mother into making a decision she might not think is the best for her situation. That goes the other way too. If a young woman feels like she was forced into choosing adoption, there would be a good chance the experience will always haunt her.

Once a young lady has made up her mind to place a child for adoption, the pressures from other people do not disappear. With so many people waiting to adopt, and with so few babies, as soon as word gets out about her situation people often start to swarm her. All of a sudden it seems like everybody who knows her also knows a couple who is waiting to adopt. They tell her that she's an answer to their prayers. They put on their best face and talk about all the wonderful qualities their childless friends have. It is a difficult balance for people on our side of the fence to find since adoptive couples do need to be active in marketing themselves in order to get chosen. Still, I've watched pregnant women squirm at the uncomfortable pressure. It seems to be especially uncomfortable for the women who are still undecided about adoption.

Everybody knows about adoption, but not everybody understands open adoption. If they did, how many people would make a different choice? If they knew that they would not have to say good-bye forever to the child growing inside of them, would they choose something different? If they knew they could change the life of a couple like Jammie and me, would they make a different choice? That is why Jammie and I are standing as tall as we can. We are not out there to tell everybody with an unexpected pregnancy that they should choose adoption, but we are doing our best to help everyone see the new option for open adoption.

Having an open adoption means that we have unique branches on our family tree. Having this unusual family tree means we get to learn new ways to love. We love what open adoption has brought to our home.

Ira is my son. I do not doubt that for a second. I don't care that he doesn't have my genes. It doesn't matter to me if he looks like me or not. Ira is my son. Taking second place only to the day when Jammie and I got married, Ira is the best thing to have ever happened to me, and it was all made possible by a beautiful young mother who was willing to look beyond what she wanted for herself. I know he's my son because I can feel it inside of me. I do not know what it is like to have a biological child, but I do not hesitate to say that I could not possibly love him more if he shared my DNA. I love watching Ira grow. I love watching his personality develop. I love everything about him. I love my son more than he will ever know until he has a child of his own.

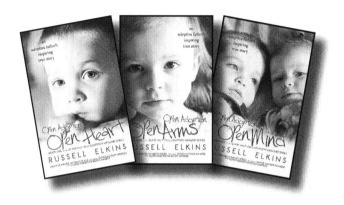

the *GLASS HALF-FULL ADOPTION MEMOIRS* *series:*

Open Adoption, Open Heart
the story of Rusell and Jammie's first adoption

Open Adoption, Open Arms
the story of Russell and Jammie's second adoption

Open Adoption, Open Mind
an interesting addition to Russell and Jammie's story
six years down the road

Russell and Jammie's Adoption Profile letter:

We can't begin to tell you how much love and respect we have for every birth parent who makes that difficult decision to place a child for adoption. We have been unable to have our own children, so we're incredibly grateful for people like you who are willing to help us realize that dream. Thank you for making that decision, and thank you for taking a moment to get to know us a little bit by reading our letter to you.

About Us

Our story began on a Sunday morning in church. With a little over a year left in college, Russell had just moved into a new apartment. Jammie had just moved to town a few days earlier and was staying with her parents while she looked for her own place. The timing couldn't have been any better. If Russell had moved to his new apartment a few weeks later, Jammie would have already been living in her new apartment fifteen miles away. If Jammie had moved to the area a few weeks earlier, Russell wouldn't have spent that first Sunday at church with his eyes glued to the beautiful blonde across the room. It didn't take Russell very long to have her cornered as he introduced himself and found out her name. All of the usual steps of dating and going home to meet each other's family soon followed, and before long, Russell was nervously in front of Jammie's father asking him for his blessing to marry his daughter.

113

Jammie was born in Utah. She grew up being the only girl and the youngest sibling in the house until her younger sister was born when she was 11 years old. She would spend part of the day roughhousing with her three older brothers and then the rest of the day playing on the floor with her baby sister. She doesn't wrestle with her brothers anymore, and her baby sister is now a young teenager, but it's still just as enjoyable to get together as a family.

Russell was born in Maryland and grew up as the fourth child out of six. While the Navy had Russell's family moving around a lot, he spent the majority of his younger years living in Nevada. He loved catching lizards and playing football or baseball with his siblings and friends out in the desert sand. All of Russell's siblings have moved out of Nevada, but everyone is still within driving distance and enjoys getting together as often as possible.

While growing up, Jammie's family watched rodeos and rode horses while Russell's family preferred watching baseball and tossing the ball around. Jammie's dad built saddles and programmed computers, while Russell's dad was a hospital administrator for the Navy. Jammie lived in the same house until she was 17 years old, while Russell lived in 10 different houses before he left for college at age 17. Jammie's house was mostly decorated with a country style, while Russell's house was mostly decorated with paintings and stained glass done by family members. With all of the differences in styles, though, the similarities are much stronger. Both families love to keep in close contact. Both families love to get together whenever possible to ride horses or play softball. Both families would do anything for each other, and both families love each other more than anything.

How We Live

Russell graduated from college with a bachelor's degree in Sociology and also graduated from a technical school with a degree as a dental laboratory technician. He worked for a few years under someone else before he and Jammie started their own dental lab business doing the same thing. At work in the dental lab, Russell does the majority of the work required to make gold and porcelain crowns, veneers, bridges, etc. Jammie assists in the initial phases of the crown-making process by making models of the teeth and also is very good at handling the majority of the business organization and finances, both of which she does from home. We love what we do.

After graduating from college and moving to Boise, we spent the first few months searching for our perfect home. We weren't allowed any pets when we were living in our college apartment, so we were almost as excited to be able to get a dog as we were about getting our own house. On the first day that we could move into our new place, we unloaded one truckload of our belongings and then went to pick out a dog even before we went to load up the second truck. We now have two dogs, Bogey and Mulligan, which we chose because of how good their breeds are as family dogs. Most of our friends have children, and our nieces and nephews are over all the time, so both dogs are great with kids.

Our Interests

We're never short of pictures from any event. Jammie loves photography and takes her nice camera just about everywhere she goes. Weddings or family portraits are the most common things that she photographs, but she's done photo shoots with just about anyone or anything, and they all turn out beautifully. The only problem with her photography is that Russell often forgets to take the camera out of her hands, so she's not in as many pictures as he is.

When Russell was a teenager he never skipped a day of practicing his guitar. On most days, he would come home late from working at the grocery store with his body being tired but his mind telling him otherwise. He would tell himself he'd just play for five minutes or so, but he always ended up strumming that six-string well past his bedtime. The many hours of practice paid off. Russell has a band with two of his brothers who play with him on stage all around the Boise area and are currently working on recording their fifth album.

Russell and Jammie both love to be active with all kinds of sports. Russell played baseball for his high school varsity baseball team, so when he married Jammie, she took up the sport and has played on softball teams with him. Jammie played basketball on her high school basketball team, so when she married Russell, he took up the sport too. Russell discovered disc golf (Frisbee golf) a few years before meeting Jammie, so she took up the sport and both have won many tournaments all around Idaho and Utah. Jammie discovered volleyball a few years before meeting Russell, so he took up that sport as well, and they have fun playing together on city league teams or just with other friends. Whatever sport it is, Russell and Jammie have probably tried it and enjoyed it.

No matter what our interest is, we enjoy doing it together. Jammie often comes up on stage to sing a song or two with Russell while he's performing. Russell goes with Jammie from time to time to help her out with a photo shoot. We love to spend the time together even more than we enjoy the activities itself. We are best friends.

Thank You

For four years now we have been trying to have children and start our family. We have been seeing specialists about our situation, but nothing has worked and each month that goes by has left us with more heartache. We can't fully understand everything you are going through during the adoption process, but we want you to know that we respect and love you very much for the decision you have made to provide additional love for your child through adoption.

About the Author

Russell was born on Andrews Air Force Base near Washington, D.C. Along with his five siblings, he and his military family moved around a lot, living in eight different houses by the time he left for college at age 17. Although his family moved away from Fallon, Nevada, just a few months after he moved out, he still considers that little oasis in the desert to be his childhood hometown.

Russell moved to Idaho after graduating from Brigham Young University in Provo, Utah. He is captain of his men's league softball team, die-hard fan of the Oakland Athletics, avid disc golfer, fiction writer under the name N.G. Simsion, and guitar player/singer with a band he formed with his brother called *The Two in the Middle*.

Above all, Russell loves God and his family.

Printed in Great Britain
by Amazon